Guide to

Governing the UK

Heinemann
LIBRARY

www.heinemann.co.uk/library

visit our website to find out more information about **Heinemann Library** books.

To order:

☎ Phone 44 (0) 1865 888066

🖹 Send a fax to 44 (0) 1865 314091

💻 Visit the Heinemann Bookshop at www.heinemann.co.uk/library to browse our catalogue and order online.

First published in Great Britain by Heinemann Library, Halley Court, Jordan Hill, Oxford OX2 8EJ,
a division of Reed Educational and Professional Publishing Ltd.

Heinemann is a registered trademark of Reed Educational & Professional Publishing Limited.

OXFORD MELBOURNE AUCKLAND JOHANNESBURG BLANTYRE .GABORONE IBADAN PORTSMOUTH NH (USA) CHICAGO

© Reed Educational and Professional Publishing Ltd 2003
The moral right of the proprietor has been asserted.

Designed by M2 Graphic Design
Indexed by Indexing Specialists
Originated by Ambassador Litho Ltd.
Printed in China

06 05 04 03 02   06 05 04 03
10 9 8 7 6 5 4 3 2 1   10 9 8 7 6 5 4 3 2 1

ISBN 0 431 14492 3 (hardback)   ISBN 0 431 14499 0 (paperback)

British Library Cataloguing in Publication Data
Minnis, Ivan
A citizen's guide to Governing the UK
1. Governing the UK
I. title   II.Governing the UK
337.1'42

Acknowledgements
The Publishers would like to thank the following for permission to reproduce photographs:
Courtesy of Foster and Partners/Richard Davies p21; © Hulton-Deutsch Collection/Corbis p9; The *Independent*/David Rose p24, John Voos pp17, 26;
PA News p12; Popperfoto/Reuters p15, 31,37; © Reuters Newmedia Inc/Corbis p10, 34, 38; Rex Features Limited pp18,24,32,40;
Stefan Rousseau/PA Photos p42; The Royal Collection © 2001/Her Majesty Queen Elizabeth p7; Stone/David Oliver p4, Stuart McClymont p23.
The political party symbols used on pages 28-29 are courtesy of the Conservative Party, the Green Party, the Labour Party and the LibDem Party.

Cover photograph reproduced with permission of Rex Features.

Every effort has been made to contact copyright holders of any material reproduced in this book.
Any omissions will be rectified in subsequent printings if notice is given to the Publisher.

CONTENTS

Government and you

How our government has developed

Parts of government

Democracy in action

Regional variations

Debate

Any words appearing in the text in bold, **like this**, are explained in the Glossary.

PART 1

GOVERNMENT AND YOU
What is the United Kingdom?

The full title of the United Kingdom or UK is 'the United Kingdom of Great Britain and Northern Ireland.' This shows that the UK is not just one country. Instead it is made up of four nations – England, Scotland, Wales and Northern Ireland, all coming together under one **government**.

Who are the British people?

The term 'British' is used to describe the roughly 57 million inhabitants of the United Kingdom. The table below shows what percentages of people live in each of the four parts of the United Kingdom.

The people of the UK come from a wide variety of **ethnic** and cultural backgrounds. As well as the four nationalities of the British Isles, around three million of us are part of a non-white ethnic minority. This means that Britain is a **multi-cultural** state, able to learn from the experiences and cultures of people from all around the world. The wide range of different people in the UK adds to this range of experience. City and country dwellers, old and young, rich and poor – all of us have a role to play in the development and government of the country.

The percentage of the population from each part of the UK.*

COUNTRY	POPULATION (MILLIONS)	POPULATION (%)
ENGLAND	47.8	83.3
SCOTLAND	5.1	9.0
WALES	2.9	4.9
NORTHERN IRELAND	1.6	2.8
UK TOTAL	57.4	100

*Source: 1991 census

Electing our leaders

How often have you heard someone say what they would do if they were running the country or their local council? People are always complaining about **politicians**, but sometimes forget that it is the people of the UK who elect these politicians, and we can vote them out of power if we do not like what they say or do.

In June 2001, the people of the UK elected a new Labour government. All British **citizens** who were eighteen years old or over were entitled to vote, deciding which party they felt should run the country, and rewarding them with power. Yet fewer than 60 per cent of these people turned out to vote, and fewer than half of them voted for the **party** that won. This meant that the new government, elected with a huge majority of seats in **parliament**, received the support of only around one quarter of the population overall. Turnout for council elections is even lower, so next time you hear someone complain about politicians, ask what they are doing to change things!

Making a difference

There are around eight million teenagers across the United Kingdom. Unable to vote, many under-eighteens feel that politics is not for them, but there are many ways in which you can help to change society. Here are just some of them:

>> Join a political party: all of the major political parties encourage young people to join, hoping that they will help to shape the politics of the future.

>> Influence local politicians: local authorities often have youth councils that allow young people to have their say in improving community facilities.

>> Join a pressure group: if you believe strongly in a cause, these allow you to help make politicians listen to your opinions.

>> Write a letter: it may sound simple, but letters and petitions sent to politicians and newspapers often make those in power take notice of people's opinions.

Throughout this book you will find other ways of getting involved, as well as web addresses that will help you to find the information you need to get started.

A school united

How would you feel if you found out that one of your friends was going to be forced to leave the country? This is happening around Britain, as families hoping to gain **asylum** in this country have their cases rejected by the **Home Office**. When staff and pupils at Forest Gate School in London learned that one of the students was to be sent back to Angola, they launched a campaign to keep her in the UK. They were able to draw in the media, forcing the Home Office first to delay the deportation, and then to allow the girl's family to stay.

The Institute of Race Relations has set up a website to help schools in this position. The Schools against Deportations site can be found at www.irr.org.uk/sad/.

PART 2

HOW OUR GOVERNMENT HAS DEVELOPED
The origins of the British Parliament

After the Norman Conquest of 1066, **monarchs** ruled as **dictators**. In order to maintain their power, they relied on an oath of loyalty sworn by noblemen. In exchange for this oath of loyalty, the monarchs gave land to his supporters and the church.

This system began to change during the reign of King John (1199–1216). John angered his noblemen by bringing in high **taxation**. They rose up against him, forcing him to agree to a series of demands, set out in the Magna Carta of 1215. This document was the first in a series that gradually introduced new powers to the Great Council. Kings were forced to call the Great Council's members if they wanted to introduce new taxes. The Council began to meet more regularly, and the first **Parliament** was born.

Lords and Commons

In medieval times, all European monarchs had parliaments of some kind. In Britain they consisted of two chambers, an upper house – the Lords, and a lower – the Commons. At first the Lords, the great landowners of the country, gathered to advise the King. This changed in the thirteenth century. The Lords said they could only agree to taxes on behalf of the people who rented their land, while Freemen and Knights in the shires and towns began to object to having taxes forced upon them. In 1264, the first 'Commons' gathering of Shire Knights was summoned, soon joined by burgesses, who were representatives from the boroughs and towns. Within 150 years the Commons took charge of agreeing taxation, and the Lords, the upper house, had lost power to the lower house.

Who should rule, Crown or Commons?

For the next four centuries little changed. Parliaments met and discussed the laws of the monarchs, but generally accepted their rulers' proposals. When Charles I took the throne in 1625, Parliament tried to assert its authority, denying him taxation. Charles retaliated by refusing to call a parliament for eleven years. This led to **Civil War** between Charles's supporters and a parliamentarian army in 1642.

By 1648, the king found himself defeated and placed on trial for treason – betraying the people by refusing to consult Parliament. He was found guilty and executed in 1649. The message was clear. Now the king must answer to Parliament.

The restoration of the monarchy and the 'Glorious Revolution'

For eleven years England was without a king. Parliament's attempts to rule alone were a disaster. In 1660, the executed king's son was invited to return to take the throne as Charles II. However, religious tensions were high. Charles' heir, James, was a **Catholic**, and as Charles II grew older, many **Protestants** in England began to fear that they would be persecuted when James became king.

James II became king in 1685, but his religious views were unpopular, and so the Dutch King William of Orange, married to James' older daughter Mary, was invited to replace him in 1688. Again the position of the king had been challenged by Parliament. The 'Glorious Revolution' had been successful, and Parliament hoped to ensure that the monarch could never again impose his or her views upon the people.

Parliament takes control

During the joint rule of King William and Queen Mary, Parliament gradually took more and more power away from the monarchy. When a monarch came to the throne, he or she was forced to accept a **Bill** of **Rights**. This guaranteed that the monarch could then not abolish laws or impose taxes without Parliament's consent. Elections were to be free from royal interference, and Members of Parliament (MPs) were to have freedom of speech and debate. England was still far from being a **democracy**, but Parliament was exercising greater control than ever.

The Dutch King William of Orange, landed in England in 1688.

A United Kingdom?

When Elizabeth I died in 1603 leaving no heir, the Scottish King James VI became James I of England. He then also held the title King of England, Wales and Ireland, but his realm was by no means united. Wales had been invaded by England in the twelfth century and had gradually become part of the English political system, but Ireland and Scotland had their own parliaments. It was not until the 1707 Act of Union that the Scottish parliament voted itself out of existence, and instead began to send MPs to London. Ireland kept its own parliament until the Act of Union of 1801 created the United Kingdom of Great Britain and Ireland. This remained unchanged until 1922, when a war for independence in Ireland led to the creation of the Irish Free State, leaving only the six counties of Northern Ireland within the UK.

HOW OUR GOVERNMENT HAS DEVELOPED
The move towards democracy

While debating whether James II should be allowed to become king, **MPs** split into two loose **parties**, called the Whigs and the Tories (see pages 26–29). These two groups were to dominate politics for the next 200 years. After the Glorious Revolution, **monarchs** retained the right to choose their own group of advisers, or **Cabinet**. William and Mary were careful to select them from both political parties. Their heir, Queen Anne, did likewise, but when she died childless there was another great debate as to who should be king. The German George of Hanover was invited to take the throne as George I. He favoured the Whig party in his cabinets, and he rarely attended the meetings because he did not speak good English. As a result the Cabinet chose its own chairman – the Prime Minister – with Robert Walpole the first to take the position.

A corrupt system

Although some of our modern political terms were coming into use, politics was very different than it is today. Elections were often corrupt, with 'rotten' and 'pocket' boroughs common. In 'rotten' boroughs, MPs were said to bribe their way to election, while in 'pocket' boroughs, the MP was selected by a small group of powerful men. When in **Parliament**, the MP was said to be 'in these men's pockets'. There were no strict rules as to who could vote – in some **constituencies** it depended on how much you earned, and in others on the size of your fireplace!

Parliamentary reform

Despite its rather strange political system, British society was changing at an astonishing rate. The **Industrial Revolution** had led to an explosion in the number of people living in towns. A new 'middle class' of wealthy businessmen had emerged, mainly living in the new industrial cities. This rich and powerful group felt it was not properly represented by the electoral system in Parliament. Change was inevitable, the 1832 Reform Act moving 150 seats away from the 'rotten' boroughs to the new towns. Despite this, you could still only vote if you were wealthy – there were only 650,000 voters out of a population of 18 million.

The extension of the franchise

The 1832 Reform Act was born out of a fear of social unrest, but it did not silence calls for change. **Radicals** wanted to take the vote out of the hands of the rich, with many demanding **universal suffrage** – the right for all men to vote. Later, the 1867 Reform Act extended the franchise, or the right to vote, to around 30% of all adult men. The 1884 Act raised that figure to 40%, but most working class men still could not vote, and women remained banned entirely.

The horrors of the First World War were to change this. Women had taken over the jobs of the men fighting in the war, and when it ended in 1918, the **government** felt obliged to grant these women the vote. Likewise, the thousands of working class men who had suffered in the trenches 'for King and Country' could not be refused a say in the government of that country.

In 1918, the Representation of the People Act gave the vote to all men over 21 and to women over 30, with the age difference removed ten years later by the 1928 Act. Further changes followed, until the 1969 Act eventually lowered the voting age for all to 18. Over 150 years after the 1832 Reform Act had increased the **electorate** to 650,000, those who could vote stood at 40 million. Universal suffrage had finally been achieved.

Women and their supporters took to the streets of London in 1913 demanding the right to vote.

Votes for women!

The Industrial Revolution had seen thousands of women enter the workforce, while changes in the way universities worked led to many female graduates. As the nineteenth century drew to a close, many women began to question a system that allowed them to contribute to the country's success, but would not allow them to vote for its government. The Women's Social and Political Union was founded in 1903 by Emmeline Pankhurst to demand a change in this system.

The protests of the 'Suffragettes', as they became known, shocked society. Many members who were imprisoned for damage to property went on hunger **strike** in prison. One Suffragette, Emily Davison, was killed when she threw herself under the King's horse at the Derby horse races in a bid to highlight her cause. Despite the outrage generated by such actions, the Suffragettes were able to keep the issue at the centre of political debate, and their efforts were eventually rewarded with the 1918 Representation of the People Act.

This gave women the right to vote, but only those over 30. In 1928, women finally gained the same voting rights as men.

PARTS OF GOVERNMENT
The constitution and the monarchy

The **constitution** of a country is the set of rules by which it is governed. In most countries this is a written document that explains and limits the role of each branch of **government**, and guarantees the **rights** of the ordinary **citizen**. For a new law to be introduced it must be constitutional (within the rules of the country) or it can be challenged in court.

Britain does not have a written constitution, or any single document that can be used to challenge new laws. Instead the British constitution has evolved over centuries and is made up of a variety of documents:

>> At its centre is Statute Law, laws passed by **Parliament** relating to the constitution. When Parliament passed the Government of Wales Act in 1998, setting up the Welsh assembly, it changed how the country is ruled, so has become part of the constitution.

>> International **treaties** can also make changes. For example, when Britain signed the Treaty of Rome and joined the European Community in 1973, the treaty was incorporated into the constitution, as Parliament had agreed to give some power over to the EC (European Community).

>> The constitution also includes conventions. These are rules of government that have become accepted over many years of use.

The Queen and Prince Philip arrive for the formal opening of Parliament. The British constitution has many traditions like this.

For example, it is accepted that while the **monarch** must give **royal assent** to a **bill** for it to become law, it would be unconstitutional for them not to. No monarch has refused since 1708.

>> Parliamentary sovereignty is at the centre of the constitution; Parliament is the supreme authority in the land. Under this authority, Parliament could vote to withdraw from the EU or dissolve the Welsh Assembly, removing them from the constitution.

In most countries with a written constitution, the rules remain in place until a **referendum** is held. Supporters of the British system argue that it is flexible, allowing the constitution to change with the times. Opponents fear it allows Parliament to change laws as it pleases, and fails to protect the rights of the individual.

The monarchy

Britain is very different from most modern **democracies** in that it is a monarchy. In France and the USA, the people elect the **head of state** – the President. In Britain the head of state is the monarch – the king or queen. The monarch is not elected by the people; instead the position is inherited. When the present queen dies, she will be replaced by her son, Prince Charles, who in turn will probably be replaced by his heir.

The political role of the monarchy

The monarch has limited powers within the British system of government:

>> Dissolution of Parliament: before a **General Election** can be called, the outgoing Prime Minister must ask the monarch to dissolve Parliament.

>> Royal assent: in order for a piece of **legislation** to become law, it must be signed by the monarch.

>> Appointing Prime Ministers: After a General Election, the monarch asks one of the **party** leaders to form the government and become Prime Minster.

>> The Queen's Speech: the government is called 'Her Majesty's Government.' At the start of each **parliamentary session**, the Queen opens Parliament and reads a speech that sets out the government's proposed legislation for that session.

>> Head of state: the monarch plays an important role in representing Britain overseas as head of state, especially within the **Commonwealth**.

Why do we still have a monarchy?

Most western democracies are **republics**. They do not have a monarch, instead electing a President. The powers of these leaders vary greatly. In Ireland, the President has little power, while the President of the USA is often described as the most powerful person in the world.

In Britain, the monarch is not a member of any political group, and is even banned from voting. Many people feel that this allows the monarch to represent the people without thinking of political gain. In times of crisis, such as during the Second World War, the monarchy can play an important role in uniting the people. Despite this, the past 20 years has seen a growing campaign for Britain to abolish the monarchy and become a republic.

PARTS OF GOVERNMENT
The Prime Minister and the government

The role of the Prime Minister has changed greatly since the title was first used in the early eighteenth century. At first the Prime Minister acted as chairman of the **Cabinet**, and the **ministers** who met were chosen by the **monarch** to be responsible for different areas of state. As **democracy** extended during the nineteenth century, the monarch ceased to have a role in choosing the Cabinet, with the Prime Minister instead appointing senior figures within his own **party**. Gradually, the role of the Prime Minister and the Cabinet grew, and by the beginning of the twentieth century, they had become the most important part of political decision making in the country.

What powers does the Prime Minister have?

In June 2001, the people of the UK elected a new **government**. As leader of the victorious Labour Party, Tony Blair became Prime Minster for a second term. In this position he has many powers, but does not have a completely free hand. Some of his powers are explained on the next page:

The Prime Minister, Tony Blair, prepares to meet the media in September 2001.

>> Political patronage. This means that the Prime Minister has the right to appoint his supporters to over 100 government positions. These range from the **Chancellor of the Exchequer** to junior government ministers. Having appointed them, he can replace them as he chooses. He also appoints senior civil servants, judges and Church of England bishops.

Limitations: In reality, a Prime Minister has to be very careful about the balance of the Cabinet. Important figures within the party must be appointed to ensure the loyalty of the **MPs**, and any different opinions within the party must be represented to ensure loyalty. A geographical, **ethnic** and gender mix is necessary to make sure that the entire country is represented.

>> Foreign policy. The Prime Minister represents Britain at the most important meetings with foreign leaders. At European Union Summits he or she meets with European heads of government to decide on crucial issues facing the EU. At G8 meetings the Prime Minister meets with the leaders of the world's richest and most powerful nations to help make economic plans on a global scale. In a time of war this role becomes even more important; ultimately it would be the Prime Minister who would decide on the use of nuclear weapons.

Limitations: The Prime Minister attends such meetings having already discussed Britain's position with the Cabinet. Treaties with foreign leaders must be confirmed by **Parliament**.

>> The dissolution of Parliament. The Prime Minister can decide on whether to ask the Queen to dissolve a **parliamentary session** early and call a **General Election**. This is an important and useful power, as it allows the Prime Minister to decide to call an election when his or her party is popular.

Limitations: Under the 1911 Parliament Act, a parliamentary session can last for a maximum of five years before calling an election. Waiting too long to call an election can be a risky manoeuvre, as the government may become more unpopular.

The Prime Minister's office

In recent years controversy has grown concerning the role of the Prime Minister's office which provides the leader with guidance on major national and international issues. Its members tend to be drawn from the PM's political **party** and can hold a great deal of power, while not actually being elected members of the government. They are often closer to the PM than members of the Cabinet, but are paid as members of the **civil service**, a body that prides itself in being above party politics. This has led to criticism of the role of these 'special advisers', especially from those who fear that Britain is moving towards an American-style 'presidential' form of government.

PARTS OF GOVERNMENT
The Cabinet

The **Cabinet** is at the centre of the British system of **government**. It is made up of between 18 and 26 **ministers** selected by the Prime Minister. Each minister is responsible for a different area of government – for example:

>> Lord Chancellor – responsible for legal matters and the judiciary (the name used for judges as a group)

>> Home Secretary – concerned with matters such as law and order and immigration

>> **Chancellor of the Exchequer** – oversees the country's finances

>> Foreign Secretary – responsible for foreign policy

>> Secretary of State for Education and Skills – responsible for schools and training.

There are eight other ministers who are always part of the Cabinet, and others who attend meetings when areas under their control are discussed. The ministers accept a 'portfolio,' or an area of government under their control. They must put policy into action in these areas and answer questions from **MPs** in **Parliament** during question time.

The Cabinet usually meets once a week in 10 Downing Street, London, the Prime Minister's official residence. There are also smaller Cabinet committees that meet to discuss the responsibilities of one ministry. The Cabinet plans new **legislation** and makes sure that all departments are working together, as well as discussing any problems that may have arisen. Once a decision has been made in Cabinet, all ministers agree to support it, even any who disagree with it during the meeting. This is known as collective responsibility, and is supposed to ensure that the government presents a united front to the nation.

If a minister thinks that he or she cannot support a decision, then they must resign. This is a very powerful weapon for a Cabinet minister, and can be very embarrassing for a government. Prime Ministers work hard to make sure that all ministers feel able to support government policy. If a minister is not doing the job well or has let down the government, the Prime Minister is responsible for sacking him or her. Again, this is very embarrassing for the Prime Minister, and often ministers in this position are persuaded to resign.

Question time

Prime Minister's Questions are traditionally an opportunity for the leader of the **opposition** to criticize government policy and to embarrass the Prime Minister. The Questions used to happen on Tuesday and Thursday afternoons. When Tony Blair became Prime Minister this time was changed to Wednesdays and they are now televised on BBC2 for half an hour in the afternoon. Why don't you watch them and see what you think of the question and answer session. Do you think the subjects discussed are important?

Who is more powerful – the Prime Minister or the Cabinet?

The Prime Minister acts as chairperson of the Cabinet and some of the more powerful Cabinet committees. In this position, he or she can decide what will be discussed at the meeting – the agenda – and sum up what has been decided at the end. The ministers have all been appointed by the Prime Minister, who is usually their **party** leader, so they will often feel a sense of loyalty to him or her. They also must remember that the Prime Minister can both sack and promote them.

This would seem to make the Prime Minister very powerful, but the Cabinet can put limits on this. Collective responsibility ensures that the Cabinet acts as more than just an official stamp on the Prime Minister's plans. Issues are debated carefully to guarantee a compromise that the whole Cabinet can support: if several ministers were to resign, it would cause great difficulties for the government. Prime Ministers must also be aware that the Cabinet could force them to resign. For example, in 1990 Margaret Thatcher lost the support of her party after an attack by a senior minister, Geoffrey Howe.

The shadow Cabinet

The second largest party in Parliament forms the opposition. The leader of the opposition selects a group of his or her MPs to act as a **shadow Cabinet**. This mirrors the positions of the government, with a shadow Health Secretary, Chancellor of the Exchequer and so on. The shadow Cabinet members argue alternative proposals to those of the government, and represent their party in the media. In Parliament, they confront their opponents at each of the government minister's question times. For example, during Prime Minister's question time, the leader of the opposition challenges the Prime Minister and attacks the government.

The Cabinet often holds extra meetings during times of emergency, such as the fuel crisis of autumn 2000. Lorry drivers caused chaos on the roads as they protested against high fuel prices.

PARTS OF GOVERNMENT
The Houses of Parliament

The most important principle of the British **constitution** is 'parliamentary sovereignty'. This means that there is no greater power in the land than **Parliament**. Parliament has the power to make or undo laws as it chooses, with no limits placed upon it.

The Houses of Parliament at Westminster are made up of two separate chambers: the House of Lords and the House of Commons. Traditionally the Lords is known as the 'upper house', but in practice it has much less power than the Commons, the 'lower house'. Parliament is often simply called Westminster.

The House of Commons

For the purpose of **General Elections** the United Kingdom is currently divided into 659 **constituencies**. In each of these constituencies, **candidates** from different political **parties** compete with each other to become the **Member of Parliament (MP)** for the area. Once elected, the MPs travel to Westminster to take their seats in the House of Commons. Here, they should try to look after the interests of their **constituents** and debate **government** decisions.

Frontbenchers and backbenchers

The political party with the greatest number of seats after a General Election goes on to form the government of the country, and some of its MPs will take senior positions in the **Cabinet**. These **ministers** each look after a specific area of government. The unsuccessful parties also promote some MPs to senior positions. The second largest party takes on the role of official **opposition** and puts its **shadow Cabinet** in place, while other parties elect spokespersons to deal with the same areas as government ministers. These senior MPs are known as '**frontbenchers**' because they sit in the front rows of the Commons chamber.

However, most MPs do not receive a frontbench position and so are known as **backbenchers**, sitting behind their party leaders. Although they have not been given a position of power, these MPs still have a very important role to play in making sure that **democracy** is upheld in Parliament.

FIND OUT... 🔍 >>

More about how the House of Commons works can be found at www.parliament.uk or you can write to: **The Parliamentary Education Unit, Norman Shaw Building (North), London. SW1A 2TT**

The Speaker

Only one MP is expected to be completely unprejudiced in all debates. The Speaker was originally appointed to Parliment by a royal order, but since the seventeenth century has been the independent chairman of the Commons. The Speaker, who is also an MP but does not always come from the governing party, acts as a kind of referee in debates. He or she calls each MP to speak in turn and tries to ensure that MPs stick to the rules of Parliament.

Members of the House of Commons, led by the Speaker Michael Martin (centre) enter the House of Lords for the Queen's Speech.

The House of Lords

Unlike the Commons, members of the House of Lords are not elected. It is made up of **hereditary** and life **peers**, Church of England Bishops and senior judges called the Law Lords. Until recently over 700 of its 1200 members were hereditary peers, many holding titles that had been in their families for centuries. This changed in 1999 when government **legislation** reduced the number of hereditary peers to 92. It is hoped that this will allow people from a wider variety of backgrounds to be appointed life peers. Its members are not paid, only receiving expenses for work connected to their role in the Lords.

Political parties have less control in the Lords than in the Commons. The largest party in the Lords is the Conservative party, but there are many who choose not to join any political party.

PARTS OF GOVERNMENT
How are laws made?

Proposed changes in **legislation** are known as **bills**. They must go through a long process before the new legislation becomes law, or an **Act of Parliament**. Bills are usually proposed by the **government** and are introduced to the House of Commons at their 'first reading.' There is no debate until the 'second reading,' when the bill is debated in the Commons, before being passed on to the committee stage. Here, the bill is examined in detail by a group of **MPs** in a Standing Committee, who suggest changes that could be made. These are debated in the Commons at the report stage, and MPs can suggest changes of their own. The bill leaves the Commons after the 'third reading', when MPs vote on the bill. This is not the end of the process – the bill must be sent to the House of Lords where further alterations

can be made, and it may return to the Commons. It is not until a final version is agreed that a bill becomes an Act of Parliament and receives **royal assent**. The diagram on page 19 shows how this process happens.

What does the House of Lords do?

The power of the Lords declined greatly during the twentieth century. The House of Lords debates government bills and suggests amendments, or rejects them completely. The House of Commons has the final say, so the Lords can only delay legislation. It also acts as the UK's highest court, with the Law Lords the final court of appeal.

A debate in the House of Lords. Bishops representing the Church of England can be seen on the right.

What powers does an MP have?

>> Control of the government: the **Cabinet** is drawn from the House of Commons and is responsible to it. If MPs are unhappy with government legislation, they can change it or vote against it. Limitations: rebellions against **party** leadership are rare. Each party has 'Whips' whose job it is to make sure that all MPs are 'whipped into line' and vote the way their party leaders want them to.

>> Question time: the Prime Minister and the Cabinet make themselves available to the Commons for questions. Limitations: time for questions is limited and MPs must prepare their questions ten days in advance. This gives time for the **civil service** to research the **minister's** answers, making it easier for them to avoid mistakes. MPs tend to get around this by following their tabled question with a series of supplementary questions that the minister must answer without having researched them beforehand.

>> Parliamentary committees: MPs of all parties may be members of Select and Standing committees. Select committees examine the work of the government in a variety of areas, such as health and defence, and their findings can cause problems for governments. Standing committees examine and suggest changes to bills. Limitations: the governing party always has a majority on a committee and they cannot force ministers to answer their questions.

>> Private Members' bills: MPs are allowed to propose their own bills. Important acts such as those legalizing abortion and homosexuality were introduced as Private Members' bills. Limitations: MPs are **balloted** and only twenty can introduce a Private Members' bill during each parliamentary session. The time allowed to debate these bills is limited, so it is rare for them to make it through the legislative progress.

From bill to Act of Parliament

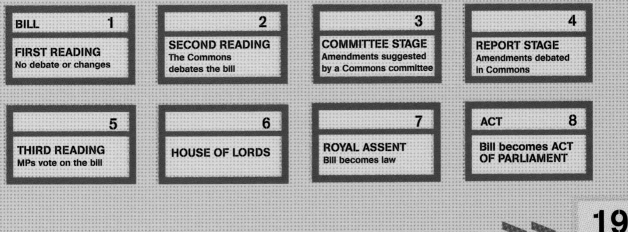

1 BILL	2	3	4
FIRST READING No debate or changes	**SECOND READING** The Commons debates the bill	**COMMITTEE STAGE** Amendments suggested by a Commons committee	**REPORT STAGE** Amendments debated in Commons

5	6	7	8 ACT
THIRD READING MPs vote on the bill	**HOUSE OF LORDS**	**ROYAL ASSENT** Bill becomes law	**Bill becomes ACT OF PARLIAMENT**

PARTS OF GOVERNMENT
Local government

If your local area needed a new bus stop, to whom would you write? Should your MP raise the matter in the House of Commons, or would it be the responsibility of the Ministry of Transport? The answer is to ask your local councillor, an elected official who helps to organize public services in your area. Without local **government** it would be impossible to govern the country. Instead of discussing the wider issues that affect our lives, time in the Commons would be taken up discussing bus stops, play areas and rubbish collection.

What does local government do?

The nature and powers of local government in your area will vary greatly depending upon where you live:

>> London: local government in London changed greatly in 2000 when it became the first British city to have a directly elected mayor. The mayor heads the Greater London Authority (GLA), which is responsible for areas such as transport, policing, the fire service, economic development and the environment. The GLA works alongside 33 borough councils that have similar functions to the metropolitan (see below) councils elsewhere in the UK.

>> Unitary authorities: also called metropolitan councils, these look after public services in the major cities of England, and in cities and rural areas in Wales. They have wide-ranging powers, including responsibility for education, social services, housing and rubbish collection.

>> Rural areas: these have a three-tier system of local government. At the top are county councils, responsible for policing, the fire service, roads and social services. These are subdivided into district councils that administer housing, town planning, leisure facilities and rubbish collection. On a third level are town and parish councils that control more basic services like footpaths and street lighting.

>> Scotland: until the **devolved parliament** was set up in 1999, Scotland had 'unitary authorities' with powers similar to England and Wales. Although these still remain in place, there has inevitably been a crossover in powers with the new parliament.

>> Northern Ireland: the violence of 'the troubles' in Northern Ireland led to Northern Irish councils being granted much less power than in the rest of the UK. Government feared that councils would be too divided to provide effective services. Power has now transferred to local **politicians** through the devolved assembly, with the councils retaining similar powers to district councils in England.

The future of local government

The introduction of an elected mayor and the GLA in London led to calls for similar arrangements for other English cities. The 2000 Local Government Act provided three options for councils:

>> An elected mayor and a **cabinet** of councillors appointed by the mayor

>> A leader and a cabinet of councillors appointed by the leader or the council

>> An elected mayor and a council manager appointed by the council.

The central government hopes that its proposals will make local government more modern, allowing decisions to be made quickly by a team that is clearly identifiable to the people.

Funding and electing local government

Local government employs over two million people in the UK, including teachers, road sweepers, police officers and rubbish collectors. This obviously requires massive funding. Much of this comes from central government at Westminster, but councils also raise their own funding through the council tax. Every adult in the area must pay a charge set by the council, with an additional charge added according to how much his or her property is worth.

London has an elected Mayor and Cabinet of councillors, appointed by the Mayor. This picture shows an artist's impression of how the new Mayor's building will look.

Council elections must be held every four years, with all of the major national **parties** fielding **candidates**. Independent candidates are common and 49 per cent of rural councillors who get elected are unopposed, so there are plenty of opportunities to get involved in local politics.

Local government in Bradford

Bradford City Council services a population of almost 500,000 people from a wide variety of **ethnic** backgrounds. Nearly 20 per cent of the population come from ethnic minorities, a figure reflected on the council itself. The council provides a good example of how all the people of a city can get involved in local government. In preparation for the changes required by the Local Government Act, the council has embarked on a wide-ranging consultation process. This allows neighbourhood forums, community groups, Year 11 school pupils and youth clubs to have their say in how the city will be run in the future. Changes in public services are also preceded by local consultation, and **citizens** are given time to quiz councillors during their meetings. More information about the services and organization of Bradford Council can be found at www.bradford.gov.uk.

PARTS OF GOVERNMENT
The influence of Europe

The European Economic Community (EEC) was set up in 1957 to promote trade between member states. It also hoped to develop institutions that would coordinate economic and social policy, allowing Europe to be managed as a single unit. After much debate, the UK joined the Community in 1973 and as its influence over the country's **government** has increased, it has been a controversial issue in British politics. In December 1991, the Maastricht **Treaty** promised closer links between the member states of the Community, and the European Community became the European Union (EU).

The institutions of the European Union

>> The European Council: this is made up of the **heads of state** of all member states. They meet to make long term plans for the EU, such as accepting new members.

>> The Council of **Ministers**: this is at the centre of all policy decisions taken in Europe. Its General Council is made up of the Foreign Ministers from each state, with votes allocated according to the population of each state. It meets to plan the policies that will put the plans of the European Council into action.

>> The European Commission: Commission members are nominated

by the member states, but once in position they are expected to put the EU before their home country's self-interest. It helps to plan the future development of the EU, putting its plans to the Council of Ministers.

>> The European **Parliament**: the 626 Members of the European Parliament (MEPs) are elected from the member states. The number of MEPs each country has depends upon its population; the UK has 87. Unlike the Parliament of the UK, it cannot reject the proposals of the Commission, but only propose amendments, which the Commission can reject.

>> The European Court of Justice: each member state appoints a judge to the European Court of Justice. Legal decisions taken in any member state can be challenged here, forcing all governments to make sure their domestic laws do not go against those of Europe.

How does the EU affect the UK?

The EU has had a great impact on the way the UK is run. When the British Parliament passed the European Communities Act in 1972, it accepted that laws passed in Europe would be more important than those passed in the UK. Removing trade barriers and tariffs has meant that Europe has become the most important market for British goods. In 1973, only 30 per cent of Britain's exports went to EU member states, but by 1997 this had risen to 57 per cent, making withdrawing from the EU potentially disastrous. The EU has opened up many opportunities for the **citizens** of the UK. Freedom of movement between EU states allow citizens to work anywhere within the EU and travel without the need for **visas**. European funding is also available for a wide range of community-based projects in the poorer areas of the country.

The decision to incorporate the European Convention on **Human Rights** into British law has allowed British citizens to challenge the government in British courts – previously, they had to travel to the European Court of Justice.

The European debate

Since the UK joined the European Community in 1973, its powers have grown greatly. For many, especially in the Conservative party, the EU has moved in a direction which is aimed at creating a 'United States of Europe', gradually getting rid of the independent power of the member states. Others feel that a more united Europe will lead to improved prosperity for the people of the continent. The problem is perhaps best illustrated by the example of the European Single Currency, the **Euro**:

>> For many, joining the Euro would be a step too far for the UK. Financial planning would be conducted in Europe and Britain would lose its economic independence. This would cause hardship, as economic policies that suit one part of Europe would not necessarily suit the UK.

>> Supporters of the Euro argue that Britain's industries would benefit from membership. They could be sure of the **exchange rate**, allowing better planning and improving their competitiveness.

>> Others feel that the UK should see the effect of the Euro on other countries before making a decision.

DEMOCRACY IN ACTION
What is democracy?

In ancient Greece, the **citizens** of a city-state would meet regularly to decide on how their state would be run. This system was known as *demokratia*, from demos (people) and kratos (rule). This would be impossible in modern Britain; 58 million people cannot meet and make decisions! In our **democracy**, we elect representatives to make decisions on our behalf – the **Members of Parliament**. Our **General Elections** must be held at least once every five years.

The campaign trail

When the Prime Minister decides it is time to call a **General Election**, he or she asks the **monarch** to dissolve **Parliament**, allowing the election campaigns to begin. Each political **party** produces a national **manifesto**, a document that sets out its plans for **government**, and summaries of this are delivered to the homes of everyone who can vote. Local **candidates** also produce pamphlets that outline what they feel they can offer to a **constituency**. Posters urging voters to support different candidates appear in windows and on lamp posts as parties do their best to promote their cause. On a national level, the leader and senior figures often board 'battle

A general election gives us all a chance to have our say in how the country is governed.

POLLING STATION

WARNING

General Election result, June 2001

PARTY	NUMBER OF VOTES	PERCENTAGE OF VOTES	NUMBER OF SEATS	PERCENTAGE OF SEATS
LABOUR	10,724,895	40.7	413	62.5
CONSERVATIVES	8,357,662	31.7	166	25.2
LIBDEMS	4,812,833	18.3	52	7.9
OTHERS*	2,473,448	9.3	28	4.4

* Northern Irish parties, Scottish and Welsh Nationalists and Independents

buses' to tour the country drumming up support. Their visits often focus on marginal constituencies – places that saw a tight result in the previous election and could be won or lost. The media plays an important role in these campaigns. Newspaper advertisements are placed and all parties with more than 100 candidates are entitled to produce party political broadcasts. These are short TV and radio presentations that allow a political party to put forward their plans.

How do we elect our representatives?

The campaign continues right up to Election Day, when the people of the country reveal which party has impressed them most. The UK is divided into 659 constituencies, each electing one Member of Parliament. These constituencies can vary greatly in size, but all contain around the same number of people, ensuring that every citizen has an equal representation in Parliament. The MPs are elected under the 'first-past-the-post' system. This means that on Election Day, each voter selects the candidate they prefer and puts an 'X'

beside that candidate's name on a slip of paper. The candidate with the greatest number of votes wins. The party with the most MPs goes on to form the government, with its leader as Prime Minister.

Other voting systems

First-past-the-post is not the only voting system used in the UK. In elections for the European Parliament, a system of **proportional representation (PR)** is used. Instead of 659 constituencies, the country is divided into 29 regions. Voters select their candidates in order of preference, and three members are returned for each region, giving 87 members in total. A similar system is used in elections for the Northern Ireland Assembly. The Scottish Parliament and Welsh Assembly are elected under another version of PR, called the Additional Member System. Each **elector** has two votes, one for the candidate of his or her choice, the second for a political party. These second votes are then used to elect additional members, chosen from party lists. This system is designed to ensure that each party gets a share of seats in proportion to the number of votes it received.

DEMOCRACY IN ACTION
What are political parties?

All **democratic** countries have political **parties**. These are groups of people who broadly agree how they think the country should be run. Together, they try to get their party members elected into power over a country, so that they can put their ideas into action.

Political parties in Britain

Towards the end of the seventeenth century, two political groupings emerged in the British **Parliament** – the Whigs and the Tories (see pages 8–9). These were very different from modern political parties. They had no central organization and were really just loose gatherings of **MPs** who voted together in the Commons.

This changed as the Reform Acts of the nineteenth century (see pages 8–9) extended the franchise (the right to vote). There were now more voters, making it more expensive and more difficult to seek votes. The parties had to set up central offices to plan electoral campaigns and attract supporters. **Constituency** party branches were added to organize campaigns locally. By 1914, Britain had the party system that we know today, with the Conservative, Liberal and Labour parties competing for the people's votes.

www.libdems.org.uk

Leader of the LibDem party, Charles Kennedy, speaking at the annual party conference, 2000.

What do political parties do?

Political parties play a very important role in any democracy. Without them Parliament would just be gatherings of MPs, all aiming for different things, making a united **government** very difficult. Parties are organized on national and **constituency** levels, with the latter giving the ordinary member the opportunity to have influence on the leadership and policies of their party. Here are some of the things that political parties undertake:

>> Elections: together the national and constituency parties select the **candidates** for **General Elections**. The party central offices produce approved candidate lists, and each constituency party selects its prospective MP. Having done this, the constituency membership is expected to campaign on a local level on behalf of their candidate. Meanwhile, the party central offices organize the national campaign; party political broadcasts, production of a national **manifesto**, TV and radio interviews and so on.

>> Electing leaders and changing party policy: party conferences are held annually when representatives of each branch of the party come together to debate policy and, occasionally, elect a new leader. The extent of how much control party members have varies between parties, but failure to listen to the members can cause great problems for a party's leaders.

>> Finances: constituency parties hold regular fund-raising events, but these make only a small contribution to the huge financial requirements of modern political parties. All Britain's political parties rely heavily on donations from wealthy supporters, while the Labour Party also receives funding from the **trade union** movement.

Should political parties be funded by the state?

Political party funding has been an area of controversy in recent years. Critics have argued that relying on donations from individuals and companies leads to parties being under pressure to favour the needs of these donors when the party is in power. This problem was demonstrated in November 1997, when the Labour Prime Minister Tony Blair announced that Formula 1 motor racing would not face a ban on tobacco sponsorship in sport. It was claimed that the decision was made because a ban might force the sport to move to Eastern Europe, taking with it thousands of jobs. However, critics pointed out that the Labour Party had just received a donation of £1 million from the head of Formula 1, Bernie Ecclestone.

Had the Prime Minister been influenced by the donation? Both Ecclestone and Blair denied this was the case, but it has led to increased demands for Britain to follow the example of other European countries and introduce state funding of political parties.

DEMOCRACY IN ACTION
Britain's political parties

Three major political **parties** dominate the British political system. Although their policies change at every election, they each claim to represent the interests of the British people.

The Conservative Party

The Conservative Party emerged from the Tory Party of the seventeenth and eighteenth centuries, changing its name in the 1830s. The name 'Conservative' is derived from the party's tradition of trying to conserve the ancient institutions of the UK – the monarchy, House of Lords, unwritten **constitution** and the unions with Scotland and Northern Ireland. The party is traditionally opposed to **radical** change, arguing that evolution, not revolution, has allowed the UK to grow into a great power.

The party is organized on three levels. Conservative Central Office is responsible for the administration of the party, while the Parliamentary Party of Conservative **MPs** makes up its representation in the Commons. The National Union of Conservative Associations represents **constituency** branches. Reforms introduced by William Hague, the leader of the Conservatives between 1997 and 2001, have given the ordinary membership a great deal more power within the party, with all members allowed a vote in the selection of their leader and candidates for election.

These changes have also given the membership greater influence over party policy.

The Liberal Democrats

The Liberal Democrat party has its origins in the Whigs, who became the Liberal Party in the mid-nineteenth century. Traditionally promoting the rights of the individual, the 'LibDems' began as the party of the middle class and business, and gradually began to press for social reform to allow the working class greater freedom. Along with the Conservatives, they dominated British politics until the First World War, when the Labour Party began to attract their working class supporters. In 1981, they joined with the Social Democrats to create the Alliance, before the two merged in 1987. The LibDems now regard themselves as the party that best represents the middle ground in British politics, although their policies are often more radical than either Labour or the Conservatives. Its members have the greatest influence in their party organization, with its party conference the supreme policy-making body.

FIND OUT...

For more information on how to join the different main political parties, go to: www.labour.org.uk
www.conservatives.com
www.libdems.org.uk

The Labour Party

The Labour Party grew out of the **trade union** movement at the beginning of the twentieth century, hoping to give the working class a voice in **Parliament**. It quickly overtook the Liberal Party, and has competed for power with the Conservatives since the First World War. Its policies fell out of favour with voters in the late 1970s, leading to a move towards the centre in the 1990s. This move was rewarded with the election into power of Tony Blair's 'New Labour' government in 1997. Many of Blair's reforms took power away from the trade unions while increasing the influence of the constituency parties. Representatives from constituency parties can now influence policy through the National Policy Forum, and also provide representatives on the party's governing body, the national executive. The election of the party leadership also changed, with each member being given an equal vote.

There are many smaller parties who represent different interests. Some represent different areas of the UK, such as the Scottish National Party, which sends MPs to Westminster but also has considerable influence in the Scottish Parliament. Other parties represent particular issues; for example, the Green Party campaigns on environmental issues.

Party policy

The table below shows the policies of the three main political parties.

Party policy in the 2001 General Election

ISSUE	LABOUR (Leader: Tony Blair)	LIBDEMS (Leader: Charles Kennedy)	CONSERVATIVE (Leader: William Hague)
TAXATION AND ECONOMIC POLICY	No change to top and basic income tax rates. Extend the 10p lowest rate band	Add a penny to income tax to pay for public services	Cut fuel tax. Lower taxes for families, savers, pensioners and motorists
CONSTITUTION	Continue reform of the House of Lords	Introduce proportional representation for General Elections. Devolve more power to regional assemblies	Only English and Welsh MPs can vote on issues regarding their country. More power for councils
EUROPE	Referendum on joining Euro when time is right	Favour greater integration. Join the Euro	Opposed to greater integration and opposed to joining the Euro
EDUCATION	Improve and diversify schools. More money available for head teachers to spend	Cut class size in primary schools to 25. Hire 5,000 new secondary school teachers	More freedom for head teachers in budget control. More parental power in school management
HEALTH	Increase staff numbers in NHS. Maximum waiting times - examine ways in which the private sector can become involved in the NHS	Increase capacity of the NHS and the pay of its employees	Increase NHS funding - by matching Labour spending plans and encouraging more use of private health insurance by removing tax penalties
LAW AND ORDER	Tougher punishments. Register criminal drug users. Deal with asylum abuse	Police numbers up by 6,000. Better victim support	Increase police numbers. Tougher sentences for persistent young offenders. Tough asylum laws

DEMOCRACY IN ACTION
Pressure groups

The role of all the levels of **government** in the UK is to decide upon and put into practice policies that cover a wide range of issues. However, for many **citizens** it is one particular area of policy that causes the most concern. These individuals often join pressure groups, which are organizations that hope to influence government policy in a certain area or to promote a certain cause. Pressure groups represent a wide variety of interests and have varying degrees of influence, but all provide an important opportunity for citizens to make their views and opinions heard. They aim to ensure that the government hears, and listens to, the views of their members.

Different types of pressure groups

It would be impossible to list all the pressure groups in the UK. There are thousands, ranging from community organizations which put pressure on their local councils, to **trade unions** trying to influence industries and the government. The majority, however, fall into three main categories:

>> Sectional groups: these represent a particular section of society, doing their best to protect their members' interests and put forward their views. Some have a lot of influence. Trade unions are capable of putting a great deal of pressure on governments on behalf of their members, while the views of the employers' body, the Confederation of British Industries (CBI), are rarely ignored. Others sectional groups rarely make the news, only coming into the public eye when their members' interests are threatened.

>> Promotional groups: perhaps the most familiar type of pressure group, these organizations are interested in promoting a particular political or moral cause, rather than the interests of their members. They include the Royal Society for the Prevention of Cruelty to Animals (RSPCA), the Campaign for Nuclear Disarmament (CND) and the Friends of the Earth.

>> 'Fire brigade' groups: as their name suggests, these groups emerge to argue against a particular proposal, then quickly disappear, often enlisting the support of other, permanent organizations. Residents' groups are often formed to fight schemes such as new roads, power stations and mobile phone masts, trying to protect their community and way of life. Others are formed to campaign on behalf of hospitals and schools threatened with closure.

What tactics do pressure groups use?

Major changes in public services, such as health and education, are unlikely to go ahead without consultation with the unions involved, such as the National Union of Teachers, or the British Medical Association, which represents doctors. This gives them and their members a great deal of influence, as such groups can cause embarrassment to the government through **strike** action and media publicity.

The less influential promotional and fire brigade groups cannot call strike action to promote their cause, and few are able to influence the government directly. They use a variety of tactics to promote their causes.

Protest and counter-protest – the fox hunting debate

Fox hunting has long been a controversial issue in British society, and a prolonged campaign against it finally met with success in January 2001, when the Commons passed a **bill** banning the sport. The League Against Cruel Sports, which had been at the forefront of the campaign, hailed the new bill as a victory. The group had organized demonstrations at fox hunts across the country, organized letter-writing campaigns and taken out newspaper advertisements to keep the issue in the public eye.

The introduction of the bill led to the formation of a pro-hunting pressure group, the Countryside Alliance, which brought thousands of people to London in huge protest marches. They, too, gained a notable victory, when the House of Lords rejected the Commons bill, throwing doubt over how the issue should be resolved.

More about the views and tactics of the two groups can be found at: www.league.uk.com and www.countryside-alliance.org.uk

Mass marches have been central to the Countryside Alliance's campaign to protect fox hunting.

DEMOCRACY IN ACTION
Pressure groups at work

Greenpeace campaigners often use the media to try to embarrass companies into acting to protect the environment.

The environment

Many pressure groups deal with issues that cross national boundaries. Greenpeace and Friends of the Earth have built up huge international memberships in their attempts to promote environmental concerns. Most recently, they have organized protests in support of the Kyoto **Treaty** (an international agreement that aims to limit the effects of greenhouse gases on the environment), trying to press the United States to sign up to the treaty. Both pressure groups have also have been involved with campaigns that may otherwise have been regarded as local protests, such as the protests against the environmental impact of new roads.

Human rights

This is another area in which pressure groups operate worldwide. In many other countries it is difficult, sometimes impossible, for people to come together to form protest groups, and those who do often find themselves imprisoned. Amnesty International was formed in 1961 to campaign on behalf of such **political prisoners**, or prisoners of conscience, around the world. They have held public demonstrations and fundraising concerts, as well as becoming involved in **human rights** education in schools. They are perhaps most famous for organizing mass letter-writing campaigns in support of political prisoners. Letters demanding their release are sent to embassies and **government** officials, making them aware that their treatment of the prisoners is being closely watched. Such letters have made an impact – one former torturer from El Salvador has said '...if there's lots of pressure – like from Amnesty International or some foreign countries – we might pass them on to a judge. But if there's no pressure, then they're dead.' Amnesty's successes clearly show how an individual can make a difference, even to a global cause.

'Fire brigade' groups

Pressure groups do not have to have huge memberships or be highly organized to have an impact on national politics. In autumn 2000, Britain was brought to a standstill by a group of farmers and lorry drivers angry at the increasing cost of fuel. The protests gained widespread support, and the government faced a dramatic drop in its support from an increasingly angry population. Disorganized at first, the protests soon became more united and consistent, with the organizers using mobile phones and the Internet to ensure their supporters were able to blockade oil refineries. Although unsuccessful in their goal of reducing fuel prices, the following year's **Budget** saw no increase in fuel taxes, a move which had been against previous government policy.

Using the democratic process

UK elections at both local and national level are dominated by the major **parties**, but often **candidates** stand to publicize a particular cause. The Green Party, which campaigns on environmental issues, has had limited success in elections, gaining several council seats and good support in European elections. At **General Elections** however, the national political parties have tended to squeeze out the pressure group parties. One notable exception in the 2001 election was Dr Richard Taylor who stood in the Wyre Forest **constituency**. Dr Taylor stood on a single issue, the running down of Kidderminster Hospital, and successfully defeated the sitting Labour **MP**, clearly showing the impact that 'fire brigade' groups can have on national politics.

FIND OUT...

What are the issues that you feel strongly about? Are you worried about the effect we are having on our environment? Do you want to speak out against cruelty towards animals? There is probably a pressure group that can help you find out more about the issue and represent your views.

You can find out more about the pressure groups discussed here by looking at their web sites.

Try the following:
www.foeeurope.org
www.greenpeace.org.uk
www.amnesty.org
www.peoples-fuel-lobby.co.uk
www.healthconcern.org.uk
www.greenparty.org.uk
www.scottishgreens.org.uk

REGIONAL VARIATIONS
Wales

Devolution

The Acts of Union of 1707 and 1801 meant that all parts of the UK were governed directly from Westminster. Scottish, Welsh and Northern Irish **politicians** had to travel to London to add their voices to the debates in **Parliament**. Recently this changed. **Devolution** has meant that separate parliaments have been created for the 'Celtic nations'. Power has been transferred away from Westminster, and local politicians have begun to make decisions for their people. How did this come about?

Wales has been ruled from London for nearly 800 years, but has always maintained a clear national identity. Many people, including the Welsh **Nationalist Party**, Plaid Cymru, have argued that the Westminster Parliament is dominated by English MPs who cannot look after the interests of the Welsh. As a result, they said, Welsh culture and language were suffering, and decisions were being made to suit English, not Welsh, needs. In 1997, the new Labour **government** accepted these arguments, and put forward plans to devolve powers to Wales. In September 1997, a **referendum** was held, in which the Welsh people narrowly supported the proposals, with 50.3 per cent voting in favour of a separate Welsh parliament. The way was open for the creation of a new National Assembly.

Welsh Nationalism has often been focused on the International Rugby team.

How was the Assembly elected?

The first election was held in May 1999 with 60 seats available. The election process is different from UK **General Elections**. Each member of the **electorate** has two votes. The first is used to select a **constituency** member in the same way as Westminster elections, and 40 members are elected in this way. The second vote goes into one of five regional counts under the Additional Member System, a form of **proportional representation**. The top four **candidates** are elected from each region.

The new National Assembly met to elect its First **Minister** on 12 May 1999. In turn, the First Minister selected his Assembly **cabinet**, with ministers responsible for many of the things that Westminster had previously controlled. These powers came into force on 1 July 1999.

What powers does the Welsh Assembly have?

The 1998 Government of Wales Act devolved several powers to the new Assembly; others were kept by Westminster. The Assembly is responsible for a wide range of domestic affairs, but only those that affect Wales. Westminster has kept control of primary **legislation** – for example, it might say that all schools should follow a national curriculum. The Assembly controls how that plan is put into action – through secondary legislation, it would be able to decide what subjects this curriculum would have in Wales. Importantly, the Welsh Assembly receives a **Budget** to spend on its domestic services as it chooses, but it cannot raise or lower **taxation**. Some of the areas the Assembly is responsible for are:

>> Agriculture and the environment

>> Economic development and transport

>> Health and the health service

>> Education, culture and the Welsh language

>> Housing and town planning.

These powers allow members of the Welsh Assembly to make important decisions that affect the Welsh people. They direct funding for hospitals and schools, work to attract and support business and balance the needs of industry with those of the environment.

Plaid Cymru

Plaid Cymru was set up in 1925 to campaign for Welsh independence. It first attracted support in rural, Welsh-speaking areas, but seemed doomed to failure when a vote in 1979 rejected devolution. The long period of Conservative government between 1979 and 1995 revived its fortunes. Wales was a traditional Labour stronghold, and its people felt increasingly isolated from a mainly English administration. Support for both Plaid Cymru and devolution grew, with the party winning four seats in the 1997 General Election. Although disappointed by the closeness of the 1997 referendum, the party bounced back to win 17 of the 60 seats in the new Assembly.

FIND OUT... 🔍 >>

Find out more about the Welsh political parties and their attitudes to devolution:

The National Assembly:
www.wales.gov.uk

Plaid Cymru:
www.plaidcymru.org

The Welsh Labour Party:
www.waleslabourparty.org.uk

The Welsh Conservative Party:
www.welsh-conservatives.org.uk

The Welsh Liberal Democrats:
www.demrhydcymru.org.uk

REGIONAL VARIATIONS
Scotland

Although the Act of Union in 1707 brought England and Scotland together under one **Parliament**, the terms of the act allowed Scotland to retain many of its old institutions, such as its legal and educational systems. This has helped to ensure that the Scottish people have been secure in their national identity and helped to encourage a desire for independence, with the Scottish National **Party** as the focus of these desires.

As in Wales, a **referendum** on **devolution** was held in Scotland in 1997, with a majority in favour – 74 per cent of the population supported the plan.

The new Scottish Parliament

On 6 May 1999, the Scottish people went to the polls, voting in an electoral system that mirrored that of Wales. 129 Members of the Scottish Parliament (MSP) were elected. Each elector cast two votes, one for the 73 MSPs representing local **constituencies**, the other to help choose 56 members from regional lists. Labour emerged as the largest party, although with no clear majority. The table below shows the importance of the double **ballot** in ensuring that all parties gained representation. Without it, the Scottish Conservatives would have gained no seats, and the SNP only seven, despite gaining 14.5 per cent and 28.5 per cent respectively of the votes cast.

Percentage representation of the major parties in the Scottish parliament, 1999

PARTY	CONSTITUENCY	LIST	TOTAL	% OF VOTES*	% OF SEATS*
CONSERVATIVE	0	18	18	14.5	14
LABOUR	53	3	56	36	43
LIBERAL DEMOCRATS	12	5	17	14.5	13
SNP	7	28	35	28.5	27
OTHERS	1	2	3	3.5	2

* Average of constituency and list ballots

Source: Scottish parliament Website

The Parliament met for the first time on 12 May 1999. Soon after this Scottish Labour leader Donald Dewar was elected as First **Minister**, and a **coalition cabinet** of Labour and Liberal Democrat MSPs was set up.

What powers does the Scottish parliament have?

The Scottish Parliament has wider ranging powers than its counterparts in Wales and Northern Ireland. Importantly, it has the right to raise or lower taxes by up to three pence, and it also receives a **Budget** from Westminster. This allows it greater freedom to develop policies and put them into action. Already the Parliament has been able to remove university fees for Scottish students, and provide a pay increase for teachers that is greater than in the rest of the UK. In addition, it controls law and order, the police and the judiciary (courts), reflecting the long-standing differences between the Scottish, and the English and Welsh systems.

A debate in the Scottish Parliament. Great efforts have been made to make its proceedings as open and accessible to the public as possible.

The Scottish National Party

The Scottish National Party (SNP) was set up in 1934 to campaign for independence. It was at its most powerful in the 1970s, with eleven **MPs** returned in the 1974 election. As for Plaid Cymru in Wales, the failure of the 1979 referendum on devolution was a set back, but the SNP, too, found its fortunes reviving while the Conservative Party was in office between 1979 and 1997. Its members were divided as to whether devolution was an acceptable alternative to independence, but they have accepted that the new Scottish Parliament offers Scotland's best opportunity for self-rule. The party gained the second largest representation in the new Parliament, with 35 seats.

FIND OUT...

Find out more about the Scottish Parliament and the political parties represented in it by looking at the following web sites:

The Scottish Parliament:
www.scottish.parl.uk

The Scottish Labour Party:
www.scottish.labour.co.uk

The Scottish National Party:
www.snp.org

The Scottish Conservative and Unionist Party:
www.scottishtories.org

The Scottish Liberal Democrats:
www.scotlibdems.org.uk

REGIONAL VARIATIONS
Northern Ireland

The island of Ireland came into the United Kingdom in 1801, against the wishes of the majority of its people. It was part of the UK until 1922, when a war of independence led to the creation of the Irish Free State, made up of 26 of the country's counties. Northern Ireland remained in the UK with its own **parliament** at Stormont.

The Troubles

Northern Ireland has a **Protestant** majority, called **Unionists** who want to be part of the UK. There is also a substantial **Catholic**, **Nationalist** minority who want a united Ireland. During the fifty years of Stormont rule, the Unionist majority always controlled the parliament. The Nationalists felt isolated and discriminated against. In 1969, street violence flared and soon after this **Republican** and **Loyalist** terrorist groups emerged.

The British Army tried and failed to restore order, and in 1972 the **government** in Westminster suspended the Stormont parliament and imposed direct rule over Northern Ireland. Despite this, the violence continued for the next 25 years, leaving 3,500 dead and thousands more injured.

The Good Friday Agreement

In 1995, the main terrorist groups on both sides declared a ceasefire, and so political talks could begin. Three years of negotiations followed before a breakthrough came on Good Friday 1998. For the first time Unionists and Republicans agreed on a way forward for Northern Ireland. A **referendum** on both sides of the Irish border followed, showing overwhelming support for the deal.

It is hoped that the new Assembly will bring an end to the civil conflict which has devastated Northern Ireland.

The agreement set up a 108-member power sharing assembly with ten ministerial departments. After an election in May 1998, David Trimble of the Ulster Unionist **Party** (UUP) was selected as First **Minister**, with Seamus Mallon of the Nationalist SDLP as his deputy. Other posts were allocated to the most successful parties. The UUP and SDLP both have three ministers; the DUP and Sinn Fein both have two.

What powers does the Assembly have?

The Northern Ireland Assembly has similar powers to that of the assembly in Wales. The **cabinet** took on the powers of the Northern Ireland Office, responsible for areas such as economic development, health, agriculture and education. It differs in its way of passing **legislation** from both Scotland and Wales, where only a majority of members must agree. In the Northern Ireland Assembly, a majority of Unionists and of Nationalists must vote for legislation for it to become law. This ensures that no side can dominate the other.

What future does the agreement have?

There remain many difficulties that threaten to break up the fragile agreement, such as disagreement about the handing over of weapons and policing. Violence from terrorist splinter groups has continued, putting further pressure on those in favour of power sharing. In such an atmosphere, the future of the new Assembly is not at all certain.

Who's who in Northern Ireland

POLITICAL PARTIES	Seats in Assembly (after 1998 elections)
UNIONIST AND LOYALIST PARTIES*	
The Ulster Unionist Party (UUP) is the largest political party in Northern Ireland. It is the most moderate of the Unionist parties and is willing to share power with Sinn Fein	28
The Democratic Unionist Party (DUP) is unhappy with the UUP's more moderate policies – it does not want to share power with Republicans	20
The Progressive Unionist Party (PUP), the political wing of the UVF, supports the Good Friday Agreement	2
Ulster Democratic Party (UDP), linked to the terrorist UDA, is against the agreement	0
NATIONAL AND REPUBLICAN PARTIES	
The Social Democratic and Labour Partly (SDLP) favours a united Ireland but has tried to promote it without using violence	24
Sinn Fein, linked to the main Republican terrorist group, the IRA, supports the right to use violence to get a united Ireland, but also supports the Good Friday Agreement	18
THE CENTRE GROUND	
Both the Alliance Party and the Women's Coalition have attempted to bridge the sectarian divide	AP6 WC2

*There are several other smaller Unionist parties with eight seats, all of which are opposed to the agreement.

DEBATE
Look to the future – issues for discussion

The British **constitution** is unwritten, so the way the country is governed is constantly developing, and could see great changes in the coming years. The next four pages look at some of the topics and choices affecting the British **government** and people over the next few years. See if you can find out more about the arguments for and against these topics.

The crowds and media gather outside the Houses of Parliament. The media have an important role to play in informing us about these issues.

Should the UK have a written constitution?

Most countries around the world have a written constitution, and for many years there has been a debate about whether Britain should do the same. A written constitution would set strict rules about the powers of each branch of government. These rules are called checks and balances. For example, in the USA, the Executive (the President) needs the support of the Legislature (Congress) to introduce new laws, and vice versa. Even when they agree, the judiciary (the courts) can declare the new law unconstitutional. In Britain, the Executive (the Prime Minister and **Cabinet**) is controlled by **Parliament**, but since the Executive has a **party** majority in the Commons, this has little effect. So long as there is a parliamentary majority for a piece of **legislation** there is nothing to stop it becoming law.

For a written constitution: reformers are concerned that parliament can make and change laws as it sees fit. They argue that there should be checks and balances in government to make sure that no branch has too much power. If Britain had a written constitution, **citizens** could challenge the new laws in the courts, and judges would consider whether these new laws overstep the government's powers.

Against a written constitution: those who wish to retain the unwritten constitution argue that judges are not elected and so should play no part in the legislative process. Some feel that judges are unrepresentative of the people – they are mainly white males, so could be biased in their interpretation of the constitution. It is also argued that our unwritten constitution has served the country well, and that arguments as to what would be a written constitution would cause division and uncertainty. If a new constitution were put in place today, it would reflect the values of today, which might restrict future generations.

Why do we still have a monarchy?

Like the constitution, the position of the monarchy has evolved over hundreds of years. Most of its role is now ceremonial, but nevertheless, constitutionally the **monarch** remains **head of state**.

Against a monarchy: for many it is time that a replacement for the position was found. They argue that the monarchy is outdated and expensive, and the fact that a royal title is inherited through birth is out of step with the modern world, in which people should gain recognition because of their abilities. Instead of uniting the people, it acts as a symbol of class divisions. Those who support this view feel that it is time Britain became a **republic**, with an elected head of state.

For a monarchy: supporters of the monarchy argue that because a king or queen is not elected, it allows him or her to stay above party politics, providing a figurehead that all the people can look to in times of national crisis. While they agree that it is expensive, they feel that more money is recovered through tourism and trade linked to the monarchy (for example, Windsor Castle and Buckingham Palace are popular places for tourists to visit). Electing a president could lead to a clash of roles and powers with the Prime Minister.

What will happen to the House of Lords?

The House of Lords has changed greatly in the last few years, with a huge reduction in the number of **hereditary peers**. At the moment, their replacements are life peers, nominated by the government and party leaders. For some reformers, these changes have not been enough. Some argue that it is undemocratic – the Lords should be replaced with an elected second chamber, which would allow some power to be transferred from the Commons. Opponents fear that this could lead to deadlock between the two houses. Others argue that the Lords should be abolished completely, leaving only the Commons governing as the elected voice of the people. However, this proposal would put an immense workload on the Commons, and remove what little power the Lords has over it.

DEBATE
More issues for discussion

PART 6

What electoral system should we have?

Britain's 'first-past-the-post' electoral system often produces results that favour the two main **parties**: Labour and the Conservatives. The number of seats the parties gain does not always reflect the number of votes they receive, with smaller parties losing out. The Liberal Democrats have often been the biggest losers under the system, as the party gains more second places than any other. The result of the 1987 **General Election** illustrates the drawbacks of the system.

1987 General Election result

PARTY	VOTES (MILLIONS)	SEATS	PERCENTAGE OF VOTES	PERCENTAGE OF SEATS
CONSERVATIVE	13.7	376	42.2	57.8
LABOUR	10.0	229	30.8	35.2
LIBERAL-SDP	7.3	22	22.6	3.4
OTHERS	1.4	23	4.4	3.5

For Welsh Nationalists, devolution is regarded as a first step towards an independent state. Will devolution break up the United Kingdom?

Mae **Cymru'n** aeddu cael llais
Wales de ... ves a **voice**

Not surprisingly, the Liberal Democrats are strong supporters of electoral reform, arguing for a system of **proportional representation**. Under the two systems of proportional representation suggested for Britain, the Single Transferable Vote and the Additional Member system, the Liberal-SDP alliance would have gained around 150 seats in 1987, rather than 22 (the two systems are already used in the elections to the **devolved** assemblies, and are explained on pages 34–39). Opponents of proportional representation fear that it would lead to weak **coalition governments** – no one party would have an outright majority, making it difficult to introduce **legislation**. Others feel that the multi-member **constituencies** and party lists required by the two systems take away any connection between the **constituent** and the **MP**, perhaps reducing the opportunity for local issues to be raised in **Parliament**.

What changes will devolution bring?

The late 1990s saw the transfer of power from Westminster to new devolved assemblies in Scotland, Wales and Northern Ireland. This has raised several questions, most importantly what role MPs from the UK's 'Celtic fringe' should have in Parliament, and whether the regions of England should also have their own assemblies. It has been argued that since devolution, MPs from Scotland, the most powerful of the assemblies, should be barred from voting in Westminster on matters that come under the power of the Scottish Parliament. For example, Scottish MSPs would be unable to influence the education system of the rest of the UK, as Scotland's system is administered from Edinburgh. It is also argued that Scotland should have its representation at Westminster reduced to only 39 seats, to reflect both its population (it is currently over-represented) and the transfer of power. This would cause problems for the Labour Party, which has strong support in Scotland.

It is also felt that devolution has left the regions of England under-represented. Voters in Scotland, Wales and Northern Ireland can turn to both their assembly members and Westminster MPs to put forward opinions, but in England there is no such local representation. Similar devolved assemblies have been suggested for England, with major cities having more powerful councils and regional assemblies elsewhere. This proposal has not met with widespread support yet. The boundaries of the regions are not clear, and the organization of **referenda** to create the assemblies may lead to some areas 'opting in' and others 'opting out.' This would lead to a situation in which some parts of England were governed locally and others at Westminster, making governing the country overall a confusing and complicated business.

FURTHER RESOURCES

This book includes many ideas for research through the websites of government and other organizations. These pages list some other sources of information that you may find useful in finding out more about government and citizenship.

Useful addresses

The Hansard Society

St Philips Building,
London School of Economics,
Sheffield Street,
London WC2 2EX.

Tel: 020 7955 7459

Website: www.hansardsociety.org.uk.

This society focuses on increasing people's knowledge about Parliament and government. It can also provide materials to help you stage mock elections in your school.

Citizenship Foundation

15 St Swithins Lane,
London EC4N 8AL.

Tel: 020 7929 3344

Website: www.citfou.org.uk.

An organization dedicated to developing knowledge of the rights and duties of citizenship. Initiatives include the Youth Parliament.

Parliamentary Education Unit

Norman Shaw Building (North),
London SW1A 2TT.

Tel: 020 7219 2105

Website: www.explore.parliament.uk.

The Parliamentary Education Unit is the place to go for information about the Houses of Parliament and the government. The Explore Parliament website has many features including an online debating chamber.

Charter 88

18A Victoria Park Square,
London E2 9PB.

Website: www.charter88.org.uk.

Charter 88 is a pressure group that campaigns for reform in the UK's government organizations.

Further reading

UK Government and Politics in Context
by David Simpson

Culture and Identity
by David Abbott

The Prime Minister and Cabinet Government
by Neil McNaughton

All above are parts of the *Access to Politics* series published by Hodder and Stoughton.

UK Government and Politics, by Andy Williams. Oxford, UK, Heinemann Educational 1995.

It would be a great help in studying this area to regularly read a daily or Sunday newspaper. In addition you can find in-depth news coverage on Newsnight on BBC 2 and Channel 4 News.

Websites

Excellent background to political issues as well as an easily accessible guide to the British Political system can be found on the BBC News Website at:
www.news.bbc.co.uk.

Another useful site providing information on all aspects of the UK government is:
www.britpolitics.com

An accessible website offering an introduction to government services and information based on where you live in the UK can be found at:
www.ukonline.gov.uk

A good overview of the political and current affairs situation, with regular updates, news features and items about the Prime Minister, can be found at the Number 10 Downing Street website:
www.number-10.gov.uk

You can read all about the Houses of Parliament, what the two houses each do and what is currently passing through Parliament at:
www.parliament.uk

Find out the latest financial news and information about the Budget at the website of Her Majesty's Treasury:
www.hm-treasury.gov.uk

For a more traditional view of our government, visit the website of the monarchy at: **www.royal.gov.uk**.

You will be also able to find out how to contact your MP or the local council council in your local area. The council will probably have a website describing local services and detailing how they spend their budgets.

GLOSSARY

Act of Parliament	a law passed by the Houses of Parliament
asylum	protection from danger, the term is used particularly about those who leave their country to seek asylum because of persecution about their religious or political beliefs
ballot	a way of voting on something confidentially, usually on slips of paper placed in a ballot box
backbencher	an MP who is not a senior spokesman of either the government or the opposition
bill	a government proposal to change the law if passed by Parliament, it becomes an Act of Parliament
Budget	the government's plans for how it will raise money for running the country
Cabinet	the senior ministers who meet to plan government policy
candidate	someone who puts themselves forward for election
Catholic	a member of the Roman Catholic Church
Chancellor of the Excheque	the government minister responsible for the country's finances
citizen	a member of a country
civil service	the service responsible for administering the government's plans
Civil War	the English Civil War was fought between the supporters of the King and those of Parliament
coalition	a temporary alliance sometimes made between opposing political parties to form a government
Commonwealth	a group of countries which used to be part of the British Empire and still retain some links with the UK
constituency	a district which elects a Member of Parliament. The UK is divided into 659 constituencies.
constituent	anyone living in a constituency
constitution	the set of rules under which a country is governed
democracy	a government by representatives elected by the people
devolve, devolution	passing power from the Westminster Parliament to regional assemblies, for instance the Welsh or Scottish Assembly
dictator	a ruler who holds all of the power in a country
electorate	the people of a country who are entitled to vote
ethnic	relating to a culture of non-British or non-white origin
Euro	the shared currency of the European Union
exchange rate	the rate at which the currency of one country can be exchanged for another
frontbencher	a senior spokesman of either the government or the opposition
General Election	these must be held at least once every five years. They elect all MPs to the House of Commons.
government	the group of ministers who decide on policies for running the country. These ministers come from the largest political party chosen by the people in a General Election.
head of state	the figure at the head of government. In some countries the head of state is a powerful position, in the UK it is held by the monarch, and is mainly ceremonial position.
hereditary	passed on within a family, from one generation to the next
Home Office	the branch of government which administers law and order

human rights	the basic rights of an individual, e.g. freedom of speech
Industrial Revolution	a period in the 18th and 19th centuries when Britain moved from an economy based on farming to one on industry
Loyalist	someone who supports the union of Northern Ireland and Great Britain and is prepared to use violence to achieve this
legislation	laws passed by Parliament
manifesto	a political party's proposals for running the country. It is put to the people before a general election.
Member of Parliament (MP)	someone elected to represent a constituency in the House of Commons
minister	a senior government figure who is responsible for a specific area of policy, for instance Minister of Defence
monarch	the king or queen
multi-cultural	a society made up of people from a wide variety of cultures and ethnic groups
Nationalist	someone opposed to the union between Northern Ireland and Great Britain
opposition	the second largest political party in the Parliament
parliament	the body which passes the laws of a country
parliamentary session	the period during which Parliament sits
party	a large group of people who broadly share the same plans for how the country should be run
peer	an unelected member of the House of Lords
political prisoner	anyone imprisoned for political acts or beliefs
politician	someone whose main career is in politics
proportional representation (PR)	an electoral system under which seats are allocated to parties in proportion to the percentage of votes they receive
Protestant	a member of a Christian Church separate from the Roman Catholic Church which follows the principles of the Reformation
Radical	19th century politicians who wanted to make dramatic changes to how the country was governed
referendum	a direct vote by the electorate of a country about a specific issue
republic	a country without a monarch
Republican	in Northern Ireland a Republican is a supporter of any group that supports the use of violence to achieve a united Ireland
rights	the entitlements of a citizen, for instance the right to vote
royal assent	the formal signing of an Act of Parliament by the monarch
shadow Cabinet	senior figures in the opposition who hold titles similar to government ministers, for instance the shadow Chancellor represents the opposition in areas under the control of the Chancellor of the Exchequer
strike	refusing to do something, usually work
taxation	the process by which money is raised to pay for government services
trade union	an association of workers who hope to protect their conditions
treaty	formal agreement between states
Unionist	someone in favour of keeping Northern Ireland's links with Britain
universal suffrage	the right of all adults to vote
visa	a document allowing entry into a foreign country

INDEX